Accelerated Learning

Advanced Technique for Fast Learning

Become a Super Learner - Learn Speed Reading and Advanced Memorization

Thomas Abreu

Table of Contents

Important Insight

Accelerated learning is an advanced learning approach that is used in many organizations today including learning institutions and corporate entities. It is research based and includes a variety of media and techniques. As opposed to the traditional laidback learning approaches where the student assumes a passive role and the trainer actively pushes knowledge his way, accelerated learning is more flexible and open ensuring that every learner is totally involved. It brings in energy and re-humanizes the learning process making it more enjoyable and productive.

Accelerated learning methods vary greatly with respect to the structure of the organization, the subject matter in question and the learners. In the words of Jacques Barzun, teaching is not application of a system but rather an exercise in perpetual discretion. The main aim of a learning process is not the method used but rather the results that it gives. Accelerated learning scores highly in this regard.

Hundreds of organizations all over the world have embraced accelerated learning and the number of those that are joining in is rising by day. This is because people have discovered that accelerated learning uses proven techniques that enable them to design programs faster, improve measurable learning and enhance the productivity and creativity of employees.

In order to be successful in accelerated learning, you need both a skeptical approach and an open mind. Healthy skepticism will enable you to rethink your assumptions to learning and at the same time enable you to maintain a balanced head even as you crunch the dazzling techniques and methods in the accelerated learning process.

Openness on the other hand will help you to appreciate that learning is a continual process and no one has seen it all. New possibilities are always knocking at your door and it is up to you to respond with an open mind. Openness will help you to appreciate that nothing is dormant but rather continually evolving. At times, you have to depart from your organizational culture and the way you do things so that you can experience the joy that comes with new approaches.

Therefore, having skepticism and openness will help you in distinguishing between the real and the artificial in the learning environment. This will in turn open up better ways of optimizing learning and enjoying even greater success in your tasks.

The high metabolism culture that we live in requires that we update our learning approaches so as to meet the demands and challenges of life. The kinds of updates that we need to make are more of systemic rather than cosmetic. We need to move from the mechanistic way of thinking that the conventional learning methods have taught us all through right from the early days of industrial economy. In the learning environment today, standardization, one-size-fits-all and behavioral-conditioning are principles that no longer produce the desired results. These principles were only effective in preparing people for repetitive and dreary tasks.

The kind of learning that will produce tangible results is to focus on creating knowledgeable workers and students who have the ability to absorb and adjust to new information. Accelerated learning ignites people's minds and enhances their psychological powers for thinking, innovating, problem solving and learning.

As you go through the chapters of this book, you will appreciate gradually that all of us are in a learning era which is characterized by genuine collaboration, total learning involvement, diversity and variety in learning methods and internal motivation. The survivor and health of organizations and individuals today depends on their ability to learn.

1: The History and Development of Accelerated Learning

Accelerated learning in the context of natural learning is a time-honored practice which has roots that go as far back as antiquity. However, in the modern movement where accelerated learning is being used to revolutionize structured learning and training, its history is not as deep. As a matter of fact, it sprung from a number of influences during the second half of the 20th century.

One of the figures whose work has been cited by many researchers is the Bulgarian psychiatrist known as Georgi Lozanov. He found out that the psychiatric patients who were soothed with Baroque music and talked to in a positive way concerning their health showed substantial progress in their healing process. His methodology known as the Lozanov approach proposes that there is an element in the psyche that is deeper than rational consciousness. He referred to this element as the hidden reserves of the mind. Following the success of his approach in psychiatric patients, he strongly felt that the same could be applied to learning.

According to Lozanov, a combination of music, childlike playa and suggestions allowed learners to internalize concepts faster and more effectively. His discovery captured the imaginations of non-standard educators and language teachers all over the globe.

Apart from the findings of Lozanov, accelerated learning has also been influenced by many other factors. Some of these factors include:

The Modern Cognitive Science

This involved research into the functioning of the brain as far as learning is concerned. It has come up with suggestions that put to question most of the conventional assumptions about learning. Instead of learning being a verbal and cognitive process, modern cognitive science has it that effective learning should involve the entire body, emotions, personality and all the senses.

Learning Styles Research

This perspective indicates that learning depends on the type of learner. Different people learn in different ways, therefore, no one size fits all. It brands it as a cookie cutter and assembly line process that does not produce intelligent learners.

The Replacement of the Newtonian World View with Quantum Physics

According to the Newtonian world view, nature operates more or less like a machine. It is automatically subservient to linear and independent step-by-step processes. With time, quantum physics disregarded this view and gave its own concept of interconnectedness. The quantum physics approach appreciates that all things are interconnected and there is non-mechanistic, non-linear and creative processes that operate within nature.

The Evolution of Gender Parity

Contrary to the early days when the society was primarily male dominated, this dominant culture is slowly being replaced by one that balances the sensibilities of males and females. This gender balanced culture has allowed in a collaborative, gentle and nurturing approach to learning.

The Decline of Behaviorism

The decline in dominance of behaviorism has opened a pathway in learning that is holistic and more human both in practices and beliefs.

The Changing Workplace Environment

The 21st century work environment is remarkably different from the work place culture of the 19th and 20th centuries. This change in environment has also affected the methods of education and training that were used before. They have become slow and obsolete and have opened the door to alternative approaches such as accelerated learning.

The Growth of the Accelerated Learning Movement

Because accelerated learning departs from the known, it has severally been misidentified as a bunch of clever techniques formulated without commitment, understanding and guiding principles. This is what has contributed to its many false starts. However, despite the teething challenges, accelerated learning has been embraced in the hearts and minds of trainers and teachers who totally agree and resonate well with the holistic, humanistic and spiritual centeredness that is brought about by accelerated learning.

Gradually, accelerated learning philosophies and methods are increasingly being accepted as the new standards for learning and teaching in many institutions including forward looking colleges and corporations. In view of the immense value that this type of learning brings to people and organizations, the number of accelerated learning students has grown tremendously in the United States, Canada and in the entire world.

Several bodies and associations have been established to propel accelerated learning into new heights. Back in the 1970s, Iowa State University led by Don Schuster, Charles Gritton and Ray Bordon started applying accelerated learning methods at the university and high school levels yielding tremendous results. Together with other people, they established the Society for Accelerative Learning and Teaching (SALT). This movement started sponsoring international conferences which attracted huge numbers of college professors, corporate trainers and school educators. It later rebranded into the International Alliance for Learning (IAL).

England was also not left behind. It formed a group known as the Society for Effective, Affective Learning (SEAL). Germany through its practitioners formed the German Society for Suggestopedic Teaching and Learning (DSGL).

By acknowledging the role played by each of these organizations and people, you are setting yourself for an exciting adventure that involves rewriting the rules of formal education. Accelerated learning produces desired results at a faster rate compared to the old methods of learning. Since it is research based, this learning system has appealed to many people and you too can embrace it as a total solution to your learning process.

2: The Guiding Principles and Barriers to Accelerated Learning

Accelerated learning is guided by a framework of underlying principles which you must internalize if you are to get the most out of this form of learning. Any attempt to go against the ideological underpinnings of accelerated learning will definitely fail and this learning approach will be reduced to mere creative techniques and clever gimmicks.

All the accelerated learning training programs including those undertaken by organizations or individuals operate based on the following fundamental principles.

Learning is an Involvement of the Entire Body and Mind

As opposed to the conventional and scientific ways of learning, accelerated learning is not merely a conscious, verbal and rational process but rather involves the entirety of mind and body complete with all its senses, emotions and receptors.

Learning is Creation and Not Consumption

The true definition of knowledge is something that a learner creates rather than absorb. Real learning happens the moment the students inculcates the new skills and knowledge into his existing structure. Learning is therefore a creation of new meanings, patterns and neural networks within your body system including the brain.

Learning is Enhanced through Collaboration

As opposed to an individual struggle and fete, learning has a social dimension. The more we interact with peers, the more we learn new things and better understand certain aspects that we may not have known on our own. Competition is not healthy because it slows down leaning. Instead, cooperation should be encouraged because it speeds up the learning process and creates a genuine learning community that always performs better than a collection of isolated persons.

Learning is a Multilevel Simultaneous Process

The process of learning is not characterized by the absorption of one little thing at a time but rather the absorption of multiple aspects at once. Good learning therefore engages people on different levels simultaneously whether conscious, paraconscious, mental or physical and makes use of all the senses, receptors and paths that lead into a person's body system. The brain by design works more or less like the central processing unit of a computer in that it undertakes tasks in a parallel rather than sequential manner and thrives whenever it is challenged to do more with less.

Learning is Best Done in Context

Learning in isolation makes concepts and facts hard to remember and easy to evaporate. If you want to succeed in learning, you have to learn on the job. For instance, if you want to know how to swim, you will excel more if you learn through actual swimming rather than getting the theory in a boardroom. The long and short of this principle is that practical is far better in enhancing learning than abstract and hypothetical situations. So as to improve the effectiveness of this principle, there needs to be time for total immersion, feedback then reflection and re-immersion.

Positive Emotions Enhance Learning

Your feelings at the time of learning determine both the quality of knowledge gathered and the quantity that you will be able to absorb. If you have negative feelings, your learning process will be inhibited. On the other hand, positive feelings will accelerate the learning process making it more effective. Stressful, painful and dreary learning cannot compare to a learning process that is relaxed, joyful and engaging. The results will be far wide apart.

The Brain Image Captures Information Automatically and Instantly

The nervous system is more responsive to images than words. This makes concrete images much easier to grasp as well as retain when compared to verbal abstractions. If you can translate the verbal abstraction into images then the learning process will be faster and the information easier to remember.

The Barriers to Accelerated Learning

Most of our learning is disabled without us knowing. What disabled it are the practices and beliefs that we inherited from the past and integrated into our lifestyles. If you look at the public education system and most corporate trainings, the traits of these practices and beliefs can be easily identified. Like diseases, they have become extremely difficult to shake off.

What makes these barriers deadly and powerful is that they are hidden and taken for granted by most of us. We tend to dismiss them as the norms and the way things have always been. Few of us question these assumptions and even fewer takes the necessary steps to overcome them. It is obvious that we need a revolution in the way we approach learning so that we can rid ourselves of these culturally imposed practices and beliefs that have made our learning so unnatural, difficult, dismal and ineffective.

One of the ways through which we can get rid of these debilitating practices and beliefs is to understand where they came from and the manner in which they found a place amongst us. The moment we unearth this, we shall no longer perpetuate them instead we shall be free to creatively construct more effective approaches to the learning process.

The following are the barriers to accelerated learning and the possible solutions.

Puritanism

The first compulsory education system which was known as the Common School Movement was the model that was used for institutions all over New England and the 19th century America. Since New

England was under the colonization of Puritans, their philosophies and influence had a profound influence in almost every institution in the New England culture. These assumptions were then embedded in the Common School Movement. This system consisted of indoctrination and discipline took most of the time thereby leaving very little for actual learning. Pain and corporal punishment were considered to be essential components in the learning process.

The association of pain and learning became so embedded in the system that any attempt to separate them was seen as a lack of seriousness. Accelerated learning is out to overturn this by replacing it with joy and freedom in learning. It has been found through research that people do best when they learn in environments that are characterized by happiness and personal interests rather than boredom, intimidation, irrelevance, stress and pain. The joy as expressed in accelerated learning refers to a deep and quiet peace complete with a sense of wholeness, connectedness and involvement. Small children are said to be the greatest accelerated learners in the entire world because they learn with joy.

Individualism

The education system that all of us have been exposed to at some point in our lives is embroiled in a culture of individualism where individual success is hailed more than communal progress. This is where the unwritten law of "Each man for himself" got its meaning from. Inspired by excessive individualism, most institutions developed with no sense of the social aspect of learning.

Education emphasized more of individual achievements and the grading system was strictly individualistic. We were taught that competing with each other for high honors and grades was the main aim of education. This approach gave rise to half-baked, self-reliant and independent individuals who were designed to operate in isolation.

This solitary confinement approach to education and training limits the effectiveness of learning. Excessive individualism and competition has cost us dearly and isolation has raised stress levels and reduced quality, speed and durability of learning. The competitive approach to learning hinders and makes learners reluctant to seek help and ask questions from one another. This disrupts the free flow of knowledge, information, intelligence and learning.

The solution to this is to get people to work in small teams and partnerships especially in projects and assignments. This has a profound and immediate effect on learning.

The Factory Model

The early schools were considered more of conscious and scientific propagators of mass production techniques. This gave rise to the assembly line schools where everything was controlled, compartmentalized, sequenced and standardized by a central office. Children were separated according to age and a curriculum was developed for each stage of learning. Every person had to adhere to the strict timings set by the administrators and anyone who defied these rules was considered not disciplined and un-teachable.

The teachers became more of production line supervisors than agents of creative learning. As a whole, the entire learning process was one huge bureaucratic system that was run like an enterprise. Schools were synonymous with detention homes and warehouses where children learned for a prescribed number of years then afterwards graduated with a certificate as evidence of their achievement.

If real reforms in learning are to take place then we have to get rid of this addiction in this factory model of education. In life, the challenges that are thrown on us cannot be tackled with much of what we learned in school. Accelerated learning helps to lose this addiction to a one-size-fits-all approach by concentrating on the ends rather than the means. As long as a path leads to the solution, it should be adopted irrespective of how different in principle it is from the conventional approaches.

The Mechanistic Way of Thinking

The 16th century brought another barrier to learning referred to as the scientific thinking. This approach emphasized the existence of two separate realms that is the physical nature and the non-physical mind. The outer world or physical realm was considered to be operated according to a certain predetermined set of mechanical laws that we can manipulate. The inner world also known as the non-physical mind was not given much attention and was considered of less concern and consequences.

Among the damages that this way of thinking brought in our society is the despiritualization of the world, excessive and competitive individualism, human alienation and exploitation of nature. The mechanistic world view when combined with social thinking brings about the psychology of behaviorism. By definition, the main concern of behaviorism is to find ways in which to manipulate our external performance just like machines while ignoring the relevance of our inner world. It makes people more of robots who can only respond within a narrow framework. It leaves people passionless, spiritually weak, emotionally isolated and devoid of the ability to think outside the box.

Accelerated learning tries to break this barrier by emphasizing a holistic and contextual approach to learning. In line with the phrase, "Experience is the greatest teacher", accelerated learning pursues the use of firsthand learning through experience rather than only learning about the subject offline.

In addition to the barriers discussed above, other barriers include the disconnect between mind and body, the male dominance which makes learning over-masculinized and the printing press approach which supports individualism and linear way of reasoning instead of a collaborative and multilevel approach.

If you are to benefit from accelerated learning, you therefore need to internalize the principles and reengineer your entire self so as to rid your system of the barriers cited above.

3: The Learning Process of the Brain

Accelerated learning is based on how the brain learns and seeks to advance approaches that emphasize on brain based learning environments. In the last 25 years, there has been more research in the brain faculty compared to all the years of human history. Up to this moment, we do not understand much about the brain and there is a probability that we never will. However, the little that has been learned so far seriously challenges a lot of our conventional educational practices and beliefs.

Brain Theories

In order to simplify and help us think on how the brain learns, brain theories were advanced. It must be pointed that these theories do not by any means give us the entire picture but enrich our understanding of how the brain learns.

The Chemical Soup Theory

This theory proposes that the brain is a chemical soup that manufactures, distributes and interacts with different chemicals so as to communicate to all its regions.

Electrical Wiring Network Theory

Here, the brain is considered as a section of an extensive electrical wiring network that is distributed in the whole body which sends and receives messages constantly. The amount of this wiring is said to be huge and the brain alone has over 100,000 miles of wiring. Biologically, this wiring is composed of dendrites and axons.

The Hologram Theory

This view of the brain has it that it functions like a hologram where all the parts contain the whole and that memory is evenly distributed throughout the system. As far as learning is concerned, this theory proposes that when something is truly learned, it is learned not only by the brain but the body as a whole. Both the brain and the body are considered simultaneous processors and not sequential ones.

The Theory of the Triune Brain

This theory whose popularity has increased over the last 20 years has it that the human brain consists of three separate and interconnected areas of specialization. These are the Limbic System, the Reptilian Brain and the Neocortex.

The Neocortex

This is considered the brain cap or convoluted cover of gray matter which consists of approximately 80 to 85 percent of the entire brain mass. This section of the brain is essential for high level functions such as abstract thought, language, problem solving, fine movement, forward planning and creativity. It is regarded as the section that makes us unique as human beings.

The Limbic System

This is the midbrain and it plays a huge role in emotions and bonding. It contains the components necessary for long term memory.

The Reptilian Brain

This is the primal section of the brain and the reason it is called reptilian is because of the fact that reptiles also have it. The main aim of this part of the brain is survival. It is mainly concerned with automated functions such as the heart beat and circulatory system. All instinctual and repetitive behaviors have their home in the reptilian brain. This brain component tends to follow routine ritualistically and blindly. It is also believed to be the section of the brain that is concerned with hierarchal power struggles. It knows how to lie so as to survive.

The Application of Brain Theories in the Learning Process

The theories discussed above play a huge role in helping us to understand the learning process and what you can do to optimize it. For instance, the traditional learning that was witnessed in the Industrial Age emphasized more on the reptilian functions which included rote learning, the teacher as the power center, repeat after me approach, the student as a routine following passive disciplined servant and a system driven by survival.

This mode of learning had little of any concern for social bonding in the learning environment. Not much effort was dedicated to teaching the students how to be creative, solve problems and think on their own. Whenever you are engaged in independent thinking, you were considered subversive and insubordinate.

Making Use of the Entire Brain System when Learning

In order to be an effective learner, you need to engage the total mind and your entire self during the learning process. By entire self, it means the body, mind, emotions and the sensory system. As you train yourself to using the whole brain, you will find learning to be faster, more effective and more interesting. You also need to keep your reptilian function of the brain alive together with its automatic functions and survival instincts. It will help you to be obedient to precedent and routine which is very important at certain times in life.

The Limbic function also needs to be involved in learning. Research has verified that emotions and common sense have a profound effect on the quantity and quality of learning. Positive feelings tend to speed up learning. As a matter of fact, there is nothing that accelerates the learning process more than the sense of joy. The preparation phase of the accelerated learning cycle has many goals amongst them the creation of positive feelings in the learner as well as awakening the social intelligence of the Limbic System. This section of the brain emphasizes the need for more collaboration rather than competition in the learning environment.

The Neocortex function of your brain needs to be exercised in order to optimize human performance and learning. This is accomplished by learning how to think for yourself, how to navigate rather than store information, how to imagine and how to create value and meaning for yourself out of an experience or piece of information.

Whenever learners have a positive feeling and are in an open relaxed state, they can easily up shift into the Neocortex. On the other hand, if their feelings are negative, there is a tendency to downshift into the reptilian section of the brain which is only concerned with survival and not learning. This downshift brings the learning process to a halt.

The Inseparability of the Body and Mind

The brain and the body are intricately linked and a movement in one affects the other. In her book entitled Smart Moves: Why learning is not all in your head, Carla Hannaford points out that the state of the brain has profound effects on the rest of the body.

Learning, thinking and memory are not confined to the head but rather are distributed all through the body. Much of the thinking, decision making and learning that we know today take place at the molecular and cellular levels.

The traditional education system which you and I have been part of separates the body and the mind. It has always treated learning as a head only affair, a verbal and rational process that has little to do with the body together with all its senses and feelings. Body movements have been found to stimulate the secretion of certain chemicals that are important in neural network construction in the mind which in turn aids learning.

Researchers discovered some time back that thinking and bodily movements are closely connected within the brain system. For instance, the section of your Neocortex that governs fine motor skills throughout your body sits next to the part of your Neocortex that is involved in problem solving. This is why your brain cannot groove if your body cannot move.

The brain and Behaviorism

Behaviorism is an exclusive aspect of the reptilian brain psychology. This is why behavior is always ritualistic, mechanical and automatic in its response to certain stimuli. Behavior is all about internalizing and repeating various programmed actions. Behaviorism as a concept was erroneously introduced as an aspect that affects the whole brain while in real sense it only deals with the reptilian section.

In our traditional learning systems, the behaviorism approach suffered a disparity with the social and emotional intelligence as well as innovative thinking because these are functions of the Limbic system and the Neocortex as opposed to the reptilian section.

The result of all this is that people were taught more on how to react in a uniform way and not how to think creatively. Training and learning in institutions became programmed, controllable, predictable and repeatable. Accelerated learning brings in the benefits of the spiritual, social, creative and emotional aspects and that is why it is considered a departure from the traditional system.

The Implications of the Brain Learning Researches

The modern theories explain how the brain works are in constant conflict with most of the traditional assumptions about learning. In order to ensure that the learning programs designed and delivered are in tandem with accelerated learning, we should:

- Create learning spaces that are stress free so that they can enhance positive feelings in the students which in turn speed up the learning process.

- Provide the students with information accessing and problem posing exercises so as to stimulate them to think, build new neural networks, make connections and create value for themselves.

- Make learning collaborative and social so as to engage more of the brain which improves the quality and quantity of learning.

- Provide opportunities and space for physical activities and movement which makes learning effective.

- Provide a real world context into which the learners can immerse themselves so as to learn with all their senses at different levels simultaneously.

4: Learning by the SAVI Approach

Accelerated learning advocates for activity-based learning which simply means getting physically involved while learning, using as many of your senses as possible and engaging the whole body and mind in the learning activity.

Conventional learning has a tendency of keeping people inactive for longer periods of time. This causes brain paralysis which slows learning and finally brings it to a stop. By getting people to move up and down periodically, the body becomes awakened, the circulation around the brain improves and all this brings a positive impact on learning.

When compared to media-based, materials-based and presentation-based learning, activity-based learning is considered far more effective. The reason behind this is that this type of learning gets the whole of you totally involved. Physical movement enhances mental processing. The motor cortex which is the part of the human brain that is involved in body movement is positioned right next to the section of the brain that is used for thinking and problem solving. If you therefore restrict bodily movement, you are indirectly hindering the mind from functioning. On the other hand, if you engage the entire body when learning, you will evoke a fully integrated intelligence.

The reason why children are such exceptional learners is because they engage their whole bodies and their senses to learn. Any attempt to separate the mind and the body, to appeal to rational consciousness only and to disregard the body hampers the process of learning. It has been observed in many people that whenever physical movement is absent, the mind falls asleep. Many learners also find it extremely difficult to fully concentrate without doing something physical.

The SAVI Learning Approach

Simply by having people stand up and move around does not automatically improve learning. There needs to be physical movement together with intellectual activity and the use of senses so as to have a profound effect on learning. This learning approach is called SAVI learning. When broken down to its components, it means:

Somatic – This is learning by moving and doing.

Auditory – This refers to learning through hearing and talking

Visual – This is learning by picturing and observation.

Intellectual – This refers to learning by reflecting and problem solving.

For you to experience optimal learning, all these four components need to be present. Since they are integrated, the best learning experience occurs when all of them are used in a simultaneous manner.

Somatic Learning

Somatic is a Greek word meaning body. It denotes kinesthetic, tactile and hands-on learning where body movement is involved in the process. Since the mind and the body are one, inhibiting somatic learners from utilizing their full bodies during the learning hampers the full functioning of their minds. So as to stimulate the connection between the mind and the body, learning events need to be created that make you to move out of your seat and engage your body time after time. In as much as all the learning is not physically active, alternating between physical activity and physical passivity can enhance your learning.

Auditory Learning

Our auditory minds are much stronger than we imagine. Even without our awareness, our ears continuously capture and store lots of auditory information. Whenever we talk, there are several significant areas of the cerebrum that are activated. The ancient Greeks may have had an insight into auditory learning because they encouraged people to learn things out loud through dialogue. The philosophy of the Greeks was that in the event you want to learn anything, you need to talk about it nonstop.

In order to optimize your auditory learning, you need to talk out loud as you solve problems, gather information, manipulate models and make action plans. Some of the ideas to help you in enhancing the use of auditory in learning include:

Reading aloud from computer screens and manuals
Learn in pairs and then describe to each other what you have understood and the application of it
Create a rhyme, a rap or auditory mnemonic from what you have learned
Talk nonstop while solving creative problems in groups

Visual Learning

Although visual acuity is more pronounced in some people when compared to others, it is string in everyone. The reason behind this is that everyone's head has enough equipment for processing visual information.

Visual learning helps you to see what a book, presenter or computer program is talking about. Visual learners are effective when they see real world examples, idea maps, diagrams, pictures, icons and images as they learn. It also helps you to create icons, pictograms and three dimensional table top displays out of your learning material.

Intellectual Learning

Intellectual refers to what you do in your mind internally as you exercise your intelligence to create connections, plans, meanings and values out of it. Intellectual can also refer the means through which the human being integrates experience, thinks and create new neural networks. This form of learning connects the physical, mental, emotional and intuitive experiences of the body together thereby building fresh meaning for itself. Whenever a learning exercise does not challenge the intellectual side of you, it appears shallow and childish. On the other hand, if the intellectual side is engaged, the problem will seem deep and mature.

To exercise the intellectual part of learning, you need to engage in exercises such as:

- Analyzing experiences
- Solving problems
- Generating creative ideas
- Strategic planning
- Formulating questions
- Distilling information

According to the SAVI approach, your learning process will be optimized when all the components are present in the learning event. For instance, you can learn something simply by watching a presentation which is visual learning, you can also learn by doing something while the learning is continuing that is somatic learning, better still you can talk about what you are learning also known as auditory learning or think through about how you can apply the information that is presented to your tasks, this is intellectual learning.

5: The Four Components of the Accelerated Learning Cycle

The human learning process is segmented into four main components which are preparation, presentation, practice and performance. Unless these components are present, there is no real learning that can take place. Irrespective of the type of learning that you are engaged in, these 4 areas are mandatory. They apply when learning how to ride bicycles, when learning foreign languages, when learning how to dance and any other form of learning.

A weak preparation phase subverts learning. This is because inadequate preparation does not arouse enough interest, harbors misconceptions and obstructs the real value to be gained from learning. A weak presentation phase on the other hand makes you passive instead of actively engaging in the learning process. In the learning process, there needs to be sufficient time for practice and where this is not available then you will not successfully integrate the new knowledge and skill into your current structure or internal organization of beliefs, skills and meaning.

The traditional learning strategy employs more of presentation compared to the other segments. A lot of the time spent in designing the learning program is consumed by the creation of presentation materials such as PowerPoint presentation, student workbooks and computer programs. For effective learning, you need to prioritize and give each phase the weight due to it. Since the presentation phase accounts only for 20 percent of the learning, you should give it 20 percent of your resources or time.

The Preparation Phase

This is the first step in your learning process without which the learning activity will slow down or come to a complete stop altogether. Oftentimes, this phase is rushed over because of the need to cover as much material as possible. This stage can be likened to the preparation of soil for planting. If the preparation is done well, then you will create a good environment for learning.

The Importance of Learner Preparation

There are many reasons why you should prepare yourself as the learner before engaging full throttle in the learning process. This is because adequate preparation will get you out of a resistant passive mental state, remove learning barriers, arouse your interest and curiosity, give you positive feelings about the subject matter so as to make you active and inspired to learn, think, create and grow as well as getting you out of isolation and into an interactive learning community.

Learner preparation also removes barriers whether conscious or unconscious that inhibits learning. Some of the barriers you will have to eliminate are fear of failure, fear of personal growth and change, indifference to the subject matter, hostility towards the subject topic, forced attendance, personal distractions and problems.

The Components of the Learner Preparation

There are many elements that you need to consider when preparing yourself for the learning experience. Some of these components include:

Positivity

You need to replace any negative assumptions that may hinder the learning process. Some of these negative assumptions may be based on the ton of material that you need to cover within a short time, the complexity of the subject and boredom. A positive feeling will make the learning process joyful which ultimately has a profound effect on the outcome.

The Learning Environment

For learning to take place, you need to move from the mechanistic and teacher-centered approach into a positive and happy environment that stimulates and inspires you to think. Invest more in out-of-standard classroom learning because it will relax and energize you. In addition to the physical environment, you also need to foster a collaborative environment right from the beginning. This will reduce stress and competition which takes the most of your psychic energy.

Clear and Meaningful Objectives

As a learner, you need to have a clear purpose of what you will be able to attain by going through the learning process. You can use pictures, words, demonstrations, examples or just about anything that makes your goals concrete and clear. This will inspire you to move on.

Total Learner Involvement

As a learner, you need to be totally immersed in the process and not as a spectator. This will make you active in the absorption of information and creation of skill and knowledge.

Curiosity Arousal

As you prepare yourself for a learning experience, you need to arouse your curiosity. The main aim of curiosity arousal is to create a natural childlike state where your innate ability to learn takes over. The childlike state consists of openness, fearlessness, freedom, joy and a sense of curiosity.

The Presentation Phase

This phase is crucial because it gives you an initial encounter with the learning material and this initiates the learning process in an engaging and positive way. If you are in a classroom setting, you should not leave the facilitator to do the presentation alone but rather engage them in every step of the way so as to create knowledge.

Remember the facilitator presentation help in creating interest, raising curiosity and jumpstarting the learning process. However, you do not necessarily need the facilitator's presentation for you to have an initial encounter with skill or new information. Since this section accounts for a fifth of the entire learning process, ensure that you spend just enough time and resources to get it going as you focus on the other phases.

The Practice Phase

This is the heart of accelerated learning and without it; no real learning can take place. In the learning cycle, practice accounts for 70 percent or even more of the learning experience. In this phase, the duty of your instructor is just to create a context while the responsibility you have involves creation of meaningful content that is relevant to the subject matter at hand. According to brain learning research, when something is truly learned and internalized, the internal structure of your chemical and electrical nervous system is altered. New neural networks, chemical pathways, associations and relationships are created. Time is of essence in this phase because if anything is not given enough time to stick, it will never integrate and nothing will be learned.

For practice to be effective, you need to promote idea sharing, collaborative approaches, trial and error, problem solving and concentration.

The Performance Phase

The goal of this phase is to ensure that everything learned sticks and is successfully applied. It is an extension of the knowledge and skill that is absorbed in the first three phases. It is more or less like the harvest after a successful agricultural season.

There are enemies of performance that you need to be wary of. Some of these include lack of immediacy in the application of skill and knowledge, lack of a support system that reinforces learning on the job, a weak company culture that does not promote new learning, lack of a reward system and the absence of consequences in the application of the new knowledge. Just as in the other phases, there should be ample time to integrate and apply all the concepts and skills learnt.

6: The Use of Imagery in Learning

Imagery is a very critical tool that helps in enhancing the speed and durability of learning. Imagery can be visual, auditory, internal or physical. It can take so many forms including body language, mnemonic devices, physical objects, metaphors and analogies, graphics as well as rhythmic jingles.

The Power of Images

Images are more powerful as messengers of meaning when compared to words. This is because the brain is more of an image processor than a word processor. In terms of size, the part of your brain that is used to process images is larger than the section devoted to the processing of words. The concreteness of images makes them instantly memorable.

The problem with the conventional education system is that it tends to be more over-verbalized thus making it grossly ineffective. It is a common practice for most of us to use flipcharts, computer screens, overhead transparencies and PowerPoint presentations that are loaded with words. Though they may seem appealing during the time of learning, they rarely stick.

If you use the right kind of images, they can help you to concretize the abstract and make it more effective, direct and durable.

The Efficiency of Image Learning

Your brain system absorbs and stores all kinds of images almost instantly and automatically. For instance, it is easy for you to remember the meal you had last evening in greater detail or the vacations you have ever had. Through imagery you can replay and relive thousands of exciting experiences you have gone through in life. The brain is more of a backstage camera that captures all the scenes in the play without the actors having to worry whether their experiences will ever be remembered. This is precisely why image-rich experiences can teach you more within a shorter time and with minimal effort.

Types of Images

Imagery comes in many forms and understanding them will open up your learning environment as far as images are concerned. The following are some of the main images used in accelerated learning.

Graphics

These include icons, pictures and symbols that help in making the abstract concrete. A good example of the effectiveness of icons is in computer screens where there are icons for recycle bin, folder, file, desktop, my computer and many more.

Graphic images help in the following:

- Depicting concepts, processes and terms in a much more vivid and colorful way. This aids memory.

- They can also help you to conceptualize the entire learning program. This can be done with a pictogram map.

- Graphic image can help in creating colorful peripherals for the learning environment which help in visualizing the subject matter.

Metaphors and Analogies

Whenever you want to grasp a concept or an idea, you can use the known to illuminate the unknown.

Metaphors and analogies are a unique type of imagery that helps in illustrating new concepts by comparing them to something that you are already familiar with. For instance, sending electrical current through a wiring network is like sending water down a pipe. You can vary the speed, volume and force through the right hose attachment and the spigot. This same concept applies in electricity.

Talking about what you have just learned is like clicking on the SAVE button in a computer. It helps you to integrate and internalize the new concept lest it disappears from your memory screen.

You can also metaphorize call handling in a large scale telephone environment to the way an amusement park works where people queue for rides.

The basic idea of metaphors and analogies is to make the complex simple by the use of natural happenings or known scenarios.

Physical Objects

Physical objects are very instrumental in helping you to make the abstract concrete. For instance, you can ask yourself: If I was to explain what I am learning to a group of people who had minimal knowledge of the concept, how could I present it to them using physical objects? This will help you to gather the objects you need so as to accelerate your learning.

You can use natural objects, toys, household items or even hand puppets to describe a process, concept or system. For instance, wearing a sandwich board with the image of a computer screen on it can help you to explain the role of a new piece of software to your fellow learners in a group setting.

Mnemonic Devices

Mnemonic or memory devices can help you to remember important information quickly throughout the learning program. Mnemonic is a Greek word meaning memory. These devices take many forms including acronyms, rhymes, acrostics, physical movements and much more. For instance, you can use the acronym ROY G BIV to help you recall the proper order of colors in a light spectrum. These colors are Red, Orange, Yellow, Green, Blue, Indigo and Violet.

The nuclear industry uses the acronym STAR to help the operators in remembering how to approach the problems in the nuclear plant. STAR stands for Stop, Think, Act and Review.

The best way to use mnemonics is come up with your own words to help you remember the concepts, processes and terms.

Body Language

Exaggerated gestures, facial expressions and bodily movements can help you to visualize a concrete picture of what you are learning. Body language has also been used widely in presentations so as to give a clear illustration of what you mean. You can use body language together with words so as to create a complete picture of the concept you are discussing.

Imagery is therefore a key component of accelerated learning where you capitalize on the brain being an image processor to help you speed up your learning process. Remember that mental imagery is much more than the things you imagine seeing. It transcends into your hearing, feeling, touching, smelling and testing imagination as well. It is effective in improving your learning performance.

7: Technology and Accelerated Learning

There is a common phrase which says technology makes an excellent servant but an appalling master. There is no doubt for whatsoever that technology has made us wealthier but it is not as yet clear whether it has made us wise. It is hard to imagine how you can function for a minute or second without technology especially computers.

What you need to realize that computers and the web are here to stay and they have a tremendous impact on human culture on many different levels. The conventional learning whose effects you are already going through has taught us that technology controls everything and supersedes any form of spiritual, emotional, social and ecological intelligence.

In as much as computers and their use in education are legitimate, they are more or less like pencils, paper and books which cannot function on their own without the human element. The World Wide Web is becoming a powerful training and education resource which is threatening to eliminate the teacher in virtual classrooms.

The surprising thing is that computer technology has rapidly advanced while the understanding of human learning has remained glued to the 19th century. Accelerated learning will help you incorporate new and mostly unconventional human learning approaches into technology.

By applying 21st century technology to a set of 19th learning assumptions is similar to automating our ignorance and allowing ourselves to get dumb faster and with greater efficiency. The bottom line here is to change your assumptions on learning from passive to active.

Limits of Technology

When used appropriately, the internet and computers can play a huge role in your learning process. However, there are some limitations that you need to consider so as to put computers and accelerated learning in a clear perspective.

Computers are Isolating

Any machine mediated learning process has from time immemorial suffered social isolation. It is easier to sit in front of a computer alone and do your things in private including learning. This however violates one of the key principles of accelerated learning that is collaborative approach.

Computers Make People Physically Passive

Technology driven learning tends to treat the process as a linear, verbal and rationalistic methodology. It does not integrate and involve the entire body in the learning process. This is the deficiency that you will suffer as learner by solely depending on computer-aided learning.

Technology-Based Training Appeals to a Single Learning Style

Not everyone can sit in front of a computer screen and learn effectively. Many of us and probably you included are physical, hands-on and non-linear learners who find computer-based learning boring, slow and ineffective.

Computers are Media-Based as Opposed to Experience-Based

Experience is not only a fundamental principle of accelerated learning but also a key component of any learning process. By replacing experience with media, technology learning becomes somewhat ineffective. The virtual space where web-based learning takes place cannot be compared to a real environment however much the two may look alike.

In order to make technology-based learning effective, you need to change your beliefs about learning to adopt the accelerated learning approach. Failure to do so will result in a waste of resources. You need to make learning more of a value and knowledge creation process rather than absorption of information.

The Way Forward in Effective Use of Computers in Accelerated Learning

As a learner in today's highly digitized environment, you could be wondering how to effectively integrate technology so as to aid your learning. Below are some of the top ways you can use technology to foster accelerated learning at a personal and team level.

Collaborative Learning

Since they are many computer-aided learning programs, you can choose the ones created for two or more people rather than picking individually targeted programs. Collaborative learning programs will help you to tap into the power of dialogue which is effective in enhancing the quality and quantity of learning.

Explorative Learning

Good computer learning programs should give you the freedom to experiment, play and explore the subject matter. In his book, The Squandered Computer, Paul Strassmann emphasizes that computer learning should not over-control the learning process but rather allow you to experiment and follow the menu prompts.

Option Rich

In order to put computer learning in its proper context, you need to view it as one component among lots of other resources. In this way, you will open up the learning space to engage other techniques that will make the computer learning approach richer.

Activity-Based Learning

Effective learning takes place when you get involved and experience real world scenarios than from presentations delivered by computers. If you are using computer training programs to learn concepts and skills, you should therefore integrate them with activity-based learning so as to complete the experience.

8: Understanding the Importance of Game-Based Learning

According to William Butler Yeats, education is not the filling of a pail, but the lighting of a fire. Learning goes beyond memorization into the acquisition of skills and thought processes that will enhance your responsiveness in a variety of situations. Learning how to think and perform under real world challenges requires more of interactive and effective field experiences and lesser of classroom engagements. This is where game-based learning comes into play.

Game-based learning draws us into environments that look and feel relevant and familiar. Experts in game-based learning say that the experiences are motivational because they allow you the learner to quickly understand and see the connection between the learning experience and the real life work.

An effective game-based environment will give you the opportunity to work towards a goal, choose actions and experience the consequences of those actions. The games also enable you to make mistakes in a risk free setting through experimentation which is important in helping you to actively learn and practice the right way to approach things. This keeps you engaged in practicing behaviors and critical thought processes which you can transfer from the simulated game environments into real life.

The Effectiveness of Game-Based Learning

Game-based learning just like the apprenticeship system has several advantages over the traditional learning model. It is low-risk and cost effective that gives learners an opportunity to re-enact a precise set of circumstances a number of times thereby exploring the consequences of different actions. Well selected and designed games will also give you a practical chance of trying out experiences that are difficult to practice in real life. For instance, you can model an explosion in a game-based environment so as to learn and understand why gas line disasters happen in real life.

How to Model Game-Based Learning Environments

In order to model effective game-based environments that accelerate your learning process, you should consider a number of principles. Below are some of these principles:

The Subset Principle

The game should be modeled in an environment that is a simplified subset of the real life environment. This will help you to map your in-game behavior to on-the-job performance. Details which are not important and relevant to the learning process should be omitted.

The Active and Critical Learning Principle

The learning environment should encourage critical and active learning as opposed to passive absorption of information. As a learner, you should not just watch the correct and incorrect ways to do things as it is with the traditional learning model but actively participate through thinking, acting and experiencing the consequences of your actions in the pursuit of your goals.

The Probing Principle

Learning is a cycle consisting of probing, reflecting, forming a hypothesis and re-probing so as to test the hypothesis and finally accepting or rethinking the hypothesis based on the outcome. When built into a learning environment, this will help you to choose and evaluate the many different causes of action with a goal of picking out the best through experimentation.

When to Use Games

Games can be used throughout the learning process in each of the four-phases of the learning cycle. In the preparation phase, you can use group-based games to arouse curiosity, measure existing knowledge and build your interest. Among the games you can use here are problem solving games, scavenger hunts and team-based quiz games.

In the presentation cycle, you can use games as encounter devices where you can access the learning materials in the course of answering the questions. Example of presentation games includes question baseball and quiz show games.

In the practice phase of the learning cycle, you can use games to practice the new skills or knowledge as well as reinforcing the initial learning. Among the games you may choose here include concentration, jeopardy, card games, board games and family feud.

Your selection of games in the performance stage should be focused on the ability of the games to help you test the acquired knowledge or apply a learned skill. Some of the games you may find useful in this phase include model building games, problem solving games, question answer games and information accessing games.

What to Bear in Mind

As a caveat, you should know that all learning techniques including games are not ends in themselves but rather a means to an end of accelerated learning. At times, a game may be fun, clever and very interesting but at end of it all it produces no long term value or substantial learning. The simple rule to use when choosing games is this: If games result in accelerated learning and improved job performance, you can use them otherwise drop them. In the words of Edward I Hall, one of the greatest faults in modern education is over-structuring, which does not allow for play at every point in the educational process.

9: Accelerated Learning by Questioning

Your ability to ask questions is instrumental in the learning process. It accelerates your curiosity of mind and the more questions you ask, the more profound the positive impact that this will have on your learning and subsequently your job performance.

In order to be a ceaseless questioner, you have to deliberately overcome the years of conditioning. As most people in the world today, you may have been unconsciously conditioned and made to believe that asking too many questions portrays you as a stupid person.

You may have also found yourself in a situation where you are too embarrassed to admit that you don't know. This drives you into a situation here you hesitate to ask questions because you fear that others may laugh at you or make fun of you.

Importance of Questioning in Accelerated Learning

Questioning is an excellent learning technique that you should aspire to have. Remember intelligence shows itself not so much in always having the right answers but in being able to ask the right questions. Questioning helps you to:

Assess Learning

By raising questions, you can assess whether the concept you have learnt has sunk deeper enough to enable you explain it on your own words. This measures the extent of your learning process.

Clarify a Vague Comment

Whether in a class setting or any other learning environment, questioning gives you the space to seek for a clarification on any area you did not understand. This certainly makes you a better learner.

To Expand Your Perspective

A subject matter can have more than one perspective. Through questioning, you will be in a position to explore the other perspectives which will ultimately make the subject matter clearer to you.

To Build Your Capacity to Support Your Interpretations

A concept can have more than one interpretation and the best way to build your ability to substantiate your assertions and conclusions; you need to learn how to ask the right questions.

To Encourage Interaction and Peer Learning

Accelerated learning strongly advocates for interactive and social engagements throughout the learning process. One of the best ways to spark discussion and communal participation is through questioning.

How to Raise Your Question-Asking Threshold

Engage Others in a Question Party

As you meet your peers, colleagues and friends, have a habit of greeting them as you would in a reception or cocktail party and then engage them through questions focused on the learning material that both of you covered or just about any subject matter. It is not mandatory that the questions you ask are answered satisfactorily. In the event a question remains unanswered, you can carry it over to the next person until you get an answer. Where a question proves to be totally difficult, you can bring in the contribution of the teacher so as to shed in more light.

Conduct a Question Marathon

So as to go beyond your question asking ceiling, you can engage in a question marathon where you ask a friend or classmate a series of questions nonstop for about 5 minutes. After this duration, you can exchange roles and thereafter all questions unanswered can be addressed by your teacher or facilitator.

Question Posting

Using post-it notes, you can write your questions on each note concerning the learning material and then put them up on a question board affixed on a wall or flipchart. You can then have your peers pick out the questions they can answer and read them out to you. This will raise your question asking tactic.

The Question Ball

This is yet another technique that will make you an effective questioner. Here, you pick up sheets of paper and write questions on them. Thereafter, you roll them up and allow your peers to pick one ball each and answer the questions contained therein. This will increase your boldness and make you a competitive questioner.

Strategies for Asking Questions

In order to raise effective questions, you need to have some strategies in place. Some of these include:

Subject-Related Questioning

When developing your questions, you should keep in mind the objectives of the subject matter or course goals. You can develop questions that help you to master the core concepts of the subject, enhance your critical thinking skills as well as your ability to communicate the ideas and facts learned to your peers.

Open-Ended Questioning

In order to gain as much insight as possible into the subject under discussion to enhance your learning, you have to practice asking open-ended questions. Such questioning accelerates your learning by opening up your thinking energies. Leading questions on the other hand limit reasoning because they suggest their own answers thereby giving your audience a limited thinking space.

Smart Questioning

Your question formulation process should be specific, meaningful, articulate, reasonable and tactical. You may decide to use a sequence of questions that gradually build on depth and complexity instead of asking a single multilayered question. A sequence of questions helps you in building a thought process that is clear and gradual. The questions should also be somehow tactical instead of plain and obvious.

Varying the Types of Questions

In order to make your questions interactive and engaging, you should mix them up. For instance, questions with a limited number of correct answers will help you in understanding and retaining the important information you have gleaned from a particular material or presentation. Managerial questions on the other hand will enhance your comprehension of the task ahead and whether you have the necessary materials to get it done. Open-ended questions prompt a multiple of options and open up the subject matter for debate and discussion. This is important in active learning.

The Bloom's Taxonomy

Benjamin Bloom came up with the Taxonomy of Educational Objectives in 1956 to provide a useful way of thinking and learning by asking questions. According to Bloom, there are 6 types of cognitive processes which are ordered based on their level of complexity. The basic proposition of Bloom is to combine questions that require higher-order-thinking with those that require lower-order-thinking. In so doing, you will enhance your ability to analyze, apply and synthesize information as well as building your comprehension and knowledge base.

The categories as identified by Bloom are:

Evaluation

This category is the highest in complexity and involves judgment and decision-based questions.

Synthesis

This refers to the combination of ideas and creation of an original product.

Analysis

This is the third on the list in terms of complexity level and involves the subdivision of the subject matter into components and parts so as to determine the motives.

Application

This category uses words like apply, interpret and demonstrate. It is problem-solving oriented.

Comprehension

This gauges the level of understanding and it dwells on interpretation and paraphrasing.

Knowledge

This is the lowest as far as complexity is concerned. It uses words like who, what, when, define and recall to enhance your memorization and recalling of information.

The quality and quantity of your questions therefore has a significant bearing on your level and extent of learning.

10: Principles of Rapid Instructional Design in Accelerated Learning

If you want better and faster results in learning, you have to train yourself to do more with less. This is possible through the Rapid Instructional Design (RID). Over the past 40 years, there has been a deliberate move to replace the traditional learning model known as the Instructional Systems Design (ISD) with a more productive design that incorporates the latest research done on the brain and learning.

The problem with the old model is that it is too slow, stiff, cumbersome, emotionally dull and linear. In today's rapid fire environment, you need an approach that is not only in tune but also flexible enough to handle the dynamics of learning as and when they occur. This will give you a better learning and performance platform to deepen your effectiveness in the learning process.

The Rapid Instructional Design brought about by accelerated learning is based on the idea that people learn best not from training materials and presentations but from experience and constructive feedback. The traditional media-based learning does not put you in charge of your own learning process and it does not encourage peer learning.

With accelerated learning, you will benefit from a learner-centered approach that focuses on what you need to do and be so as to achieve success in learning. RID will also move you through a series of exciting experiences that vary from simple to complex. Each of these experiences is followed by appropriate feedback, refection and retrial. These activities will allow you to work with your peers in a real setting so as to create your own meaning of the knowledge and skills that you learn.

The following principles of Rapid Instructional Design will accelerate your learning and make it more effective.

The Four-Phase Learning Cycle

When designing your learning process, you should incorporate the earlier discussed concepts that make the four-phase learning cycle. These are the preparation, presentation, practice and performance. Each phase should be allocated the appropriate time and other resources based on its overall contribution to the whole learning process. Presentation should take about 20 percent of the resources while practice should be allocated approximately 70 percent of the resources. When measuring your performance, ensure that you use realistic yardsticks that will reflect your level of progress on the learning process.

Compliance with All Learning Styles

Your learning design should factor in all the possible learning styles. The best way to achieve this is to use the SAVI approach. The benefit of the SAVI model is that it involves every part of you from the physical to the mental therefore giving you a wholesome learning experience.

Somatic learning takes care of the movements and the actions during learning, auditory deals with the listening and the verbal communication, the visual element is concerned with observation and picturing while the intellectual is all about problem solving and reflection. Although it is not mandatory to use all these four components of the SAVI approach in equal proportions, it is absolutely necessary to incorporate all of them to enhance your learning.

Activity-Based

In designing a learning program that suits you, your priority should not be on the materials and presentations but rather on the activities that you will need to engage in so as to accelerate your knowledge and skill pick up process. The active experiences will avail more learning opportunities as compared to the materials and presentations irrespective of how technologically sophisticated they are.

Create a Learning Community

In accelerated learning, isolation of individuals does not avail much. For you to come up with effective learning program, you have to design your learning process with a community of learners in perspective. The interconnectivity between other learners and you will bring in more intelligence.

A lot of research has been done on the effectiveness of peer learning and the conclusion reached is that this form of learning is far much superior to the other models of instruction. The learning community approach will enable you to be a learner and a teacher at the same time.

Integrate Physically Active and Passive Learning

While learning, getting up and moving around or doing something physical accelerates the process of skill and knowledge absorption. This is because such movements enhance the brain circulation making it alert to every effort in the learning process. To get the maximum benefit from your learning model, it should balance between physical passivity and activity.

Some of the physical learning activities to include in your design are talking, standing, manipulation of physical objects, creation of pictograms and models as well as engaging in hands-on activities.

On the other hand, the physical passive components to balance out are thinking, observing, building mental models, reflecting, listening to presentations and learning with computers. The back and forth rhythmic movement between the physically passive and the physically active will sustain your energy and improve your learning.

Adoption of the 30/70 Rule

As you found out through each of the previous chapters, accelerated learning is concerned more about making you the creator of your own meaning, knowledge and skills as opposed to absorbing directly from presentations and trainers. The program you design should therefore be 30 percent or less focused on media presentations while 70 percent should be devoted to practice and integration. Such a design will get the ball in your court as often and as long as possible.

Flexible and Open-Ended

The tradition ISD model has been discredited for being prescriptive, rigid and cast in stone. This is particularly manifested in eLearning program packages. For your program to work, it should be flexible and easy to modify because in this way it will be a better fit for the ever changing world we live in. for learning to be relevant, it should be a continuous work in progress and evolve with time to be in tandem with societal dynamics.

What is interesting with RID is that it reduces your training time, enhances a higher level of your learning involvement all of which improve your learning experience. Accelerated learning eliminates or lessens the contribution of your tutor and gives space for you to engage the materials yourself so that you can totally control the learning process. It makes you responsible for your own learning.

Conclusion

Accelerated learning contributes to your competence, speed and pleasure as a learner. It enables you to move beyond the assumptions of the traditional learning model which has proved to be ineffective into a fresh understanding that is geared to make you more energized, creative and successful in your learning process.

Despite the hundreds of techniques and ideas that come with accelerated learning, it is the basic philosophy of this learning approach that will spur you on and keep you going. It is therefore important for you to understand as the learner that accelerated learning is not a collection of gimmicks, clever tricks and techniques but rather a total system that enhances and speeds up your learning process.

While implementing the techniques discussed in this book, you should first understand the principles and philosophy that underlies them. This will give you tremendous success, deepen your learning experience and extend it for the rest of your life.

Accelerated learning requires a change of mind, a reconsideration of your assumptions and in some cases a total abandonment of some long held beliefs about human learning. These assumptions which have been part of our learning culture need to be jettisoned if we are to meet the challenges of the 21st century.

Printed in Great Britain
by Amazon

28142700R00046